To Louise

Blue Water Café

*Best wishes
Sue*

Sue Davies

GW00693891

Oversteps Books

First published in 2014 by

Oversteps Books Ltd
6 Halwell House
South Pool
Nr Kingsbridge
Devon
TQ7 2RX
UK

www.overstepsbooks.com

Printed in Great Britain by imprint digital, Devon

To the memory of
Sophie Chmieloviec
1919–2003

Acknowledgements:

Acknowledgements are due to the editors of the following publications where these poems or versions of them first appeared: Acumen, Ambit, Artemis, Envoi, Iota, Ireland Review, 10th Muse, Orbis, The Observer, Poetry Nottingham, Poetry Wales, Scratch, Sentinel and Writing Women.

White won First Prize in the Alan Sillitoe Memorial Competition 2013; *You are Wheeled into the Bright Sunlight* won First Prize in the Fire River Poetry Competition 2013; *23 Fitzroy Road* won Second Prize in the Sentinel Poetry Competition 2012; and *Skylarks* won Third Prize in the Poetry Nottingham Competition 2013. Commended poems include *Oxford Wedding*, *1962* and *Little Buddha*.

The Excursion first appeared in *Marigolds Grow Wild on Platforms*, an anthology edited by Peggy Poole (Cassell Illustrated, 1996). Two poems, *Flux* and *The Blue Car and the Airstream Trailer*, were exhibited with artwork in *Under the Greenwood*, an exhibition held at St Barbe Museum, Lymington, November 2013.

Heartfelt thanks are due to Alwyn Marriage for her editorial assistance; and to Peter, Daniel and Sophie for their support and help during the preparation of this collection.

Contents

White	1
Quantum	2
23 Fitzroy Road, Primrose Hill	3
Hideaway	4
Séance	5
1962	6
Night Nurse	7
Sting	8
The Day Room	10
White Trash	11
You are Wheeled into the Bright Sunlight	12
The Walled Garden	13
Easter Gathering	14
Grandmother Cash	15
Billet Doux	16
The Excursion	17
Waterfall	18
Gold	19
The Quiet Man	20
Persephone	21
Chagall's Midsummer Night's Dream	22
The Woodshed	23
Plums	24
Adrift	25
Mina	26
Miracles	27
Descent	28
Oxford Wedding	29
The Midwife	30
Little Buddha	31
Perspectives	32
Starlings	34
Moondrop	35
Gravity	36
Fear of Sharks	37
Wavelengths	38

Blue Water Café   39
Elena   40
Awakening   41
Night Watch in Prague   42
Flux   43
Aviator   44
Daybreak   45
Miranda and the Moon Calf   46
Palimpsest   47
Skylarks   48
The Blue Car and the Airstream Trailer   49

White

Taking up her paint brush dipped in indigo
Ai-Ling told me her grandmother long ago
said she was born with ink in her veins.
I can believe it. I watch her paint a perfect
square with two evenly spaced lines inside
like ladder rungs, and tip it with a stalk.
Ah, I say, that looks like an apple box.

Ai-Ling laughs without showing her teeth.
This means white, she says. In pictures
of our universe it is the shade of grief.
No luck, no colour, the tint of death.
White speech means futile arguments.
White rice is a man who takes advantage.
A white visit bears no fruit and *white walking*
is much effort but little gain.

Ai-Ling consults my astrological chart
and scowls, leading me to believe I, too,
am tainted white. I hold my breath
and hope for white lies, a sprinkle
of Ai-Ling's white magic. I tell her
I love the sound of waves and the white
noise of rain. That figures, she says,
your birth stars say you have *affini-tay*
with the moon. You are a sad, lonely,
luckless woman. But like the moon
you bring light to dark, water to drought.

Quantum

Walking down Rue Cézanne
coming unstuck in the rip tide
happening now and always

I smell the rain in the leaves
warm sandstone polished by showers
pear blossom scent wafting

down from the courtyard trees
skipping sideways I avoid the tar puddle's splash
as if my flea-bitten life depended on it

traces of you strewn
by God's indolent hand over Aix-en-Provence
pieces of light defying time and gravity

a season with no name so bright the old sun
won't need to shine now but always
chancing here and there after the day

without a yesterday
the beating of our hearts like the burning ember of bees
and a tremolo of a lark above the blue grass.

23 Fitzroy Road, Primrose Hill *

What picture smoothed the mind's eye
and brought her to life again?
Maybe the white pillow case on the line
puffed and puckered like a barnacle goose.

Or the memory of my first love
waiting for me in his room while I,
a callow, skimp of a girl – barely
seventeen and not yet broken in –
carelessly lingered by the landing
window, where below, over the fence
I saw a young mother pegging
out nappies in the snow along
a frosted loop of rope – her red hair
plaited and coiled like a coronet
to frame the loveliness of her face.

And I found myself caught in the silent
beauty and rhythm of her movement –
arching down and reaching up
on the ringing, frosted path –
her raw, worn hands pinching
the corners of her parchment poetry –
her masterpieces stretched out to dry.

I didn't know then her mirrors
were already sheeted, and her spirit
demised with every shot of breath.
And I didn't know she wanted a sarcophagus
stamped with the face of the moon –
bold, too, with tigery stripes –
her body embalmed in warm
honey to lie beside her copper cauldron
and rouge-pots glowing vermilion
like the eyes of a predatory god.
And her heart to be wrapped
in brown paper, tied up with string
and tucked between her bare, crossed feet.

* Where Sylvia Plath resided briefly before she took her own life.

3

Hideaway

At night a silence flattens –
I hear the resonance of metal

that final thud.
Now, grit smacks the window –

and even the blunt-faced moon can't get a shine on itself.
At last

the dying rattle-breath of the late train
dispersing the dark

and I'm reminded of your welcome
that afternoon when you opened the door

your feet showing the way – those downtrodden
heels ahead

pounding the stairs.

Séance

Late summer,
when the sun and moon held a truce, and spent
meadow grasses leaned into the mist,

they walked the path to escape private inquisitions,
both on the brink of something new, momentous.
He daren't touch her, only with whispers –

small talk like warm buffs of wind from the open fields.
His presence she felt completely, someone lost
in need of warmth and assurance.

And then everything dissolved to faint lines
like watermarks on paper held up to the light.
And the air thickened and clouds massed

to end the singing of birds as they sat
on the riverbank – anticipation mounting.
She knew this was the moment – an annulment

of self, watching the rings widening
on the black water and rushes bowing
with the weight of rain. Suddenly, the heat of him –

and soft wings brushing her shoulder.
Whatever left her then, he tenderly
caught, and loved back again.

1962

Between the end of the Chatterley ban
And the Beatles' first LP

What were we then
already no more than a season away from love?
Uncalled for, love stalked us –
you sauntering across the lumpy
schoolyard for lunch, and I hunched at my desk,
daydreaming of how I would become
with or without a man.

                           Through the wide-open
window, I caught a glimpse of my future –
the French teacher and his friend under
a parched sky, thoughts away from the gauche
girls in the classroom above, our necks
chaffed by starched collars, spicing
our milk with salacious talk – what French
kissing might be like, or picking up beatniks
in coffee bars, black stockings, short
skirts, padded bra, and the curse.

What planetary configuration
fixed you in London for that chance sighting –
before the winter of deep snow when
summer flushed in love's wake, and you
strolled across the globe of my eye?

Night Nurse

Alert
to your call
I hawk between beds.

Small albino faces,
friends of the moon
tucked in hillocks of bone,
grow paler still in the darkness.

Old man,
you mistake me for an angel,
your life flickering
across your terrible white eyes.

I take your cold hand
cramped on the pillow,
and fold it into mine.
Then, when it is time,
I will open the gates for you.

Sting

Once upon a time
I read you a story called *How the Bee Became*
and you cried and snuggled up at my side,
soft as a rabbit, hugging your blanket
with holes, your toe protruding
like a small, white pebble caught
in a fisherman's net, and then
I told you about the time in the garden
one summer, when your sister
punched the air with her closed fist,
calling out her warning, "Bee! Bee! Bee!"
                    Frantically, I parted
the grass, shook my skirt, searched the air.

"There is no bee," I comforted her. But then
she unfolded her clenched hand, and I saw
a tiny spear, its tip embedded in her palm,
and the angry bumble bee staggered off
on its last crooked flight.

                    *

Time has made you strong and tall.
We stood together by the window,
watching the grey squirrels racing
through the bare birches and blackbirds
zipping over the lawn. "Watching them
is addictive," you said. And then you
surprised me with lines from a poem:
            Terrifying are the attent sleek thrushes on the lawn,
*More coiled steel than living –. ***

* *from 'Thrushes' by Ted Hughes*

8

And the loneliness of your mind-dark
spread like hoar frost over your eyes,
and the acorn I meant to plant
before spring lay hollow and brittle
on the sill, when suddenly a jay
flew into the garden and you called,
Dad! Dad! Such a beauty. Come and see!

The Day Room

O, how they tore at you – your family.
Afterwards you bloomed like scented gardenias.

At night you dream-walked the air clean of them.
The ivy turned black; white phlox shimmered.

The grass quickened under your feet and your silken
scarves fanned open like the wings of a golden oriole.

At daybreak, they caught you. It was over.
You were no trouble at all. Your mother

signed the papers. There was nothing more to do.
You sit for hours by the wall in the Day Room

like a good girl, speechless – just as they had all wished –
waiting for your brother Tom to come. He kisses

your clouded eyes, bearing gifts: his latest script,
a fading bouquet of myrtle and winter roses.

White Trash

So you wear your sorrow too, big fat white mama,
sprawled like lard bags on the hospital shelf.

My black hands must tend you. I rummage
the flannel in crevices of thighs and breasts,

your limbs heavy as joists, your tangled hair,
white as hoar frost. Then I bandage your jaw shut,

knot a bow of truce under your chin, your lips puckering
like the underside of a toadstool, and as likely poisonous.

I plug your apertures and finish you off with a shroud
of talc, smoothed over stretch marks like snail tracks

on a continent of stone. Too broad for the standard
nightdress, I leave you naked beneath the sheet

among your enemies in the candle-lit chapel.
You're all earth's children now, divided only

by flame, and I stay a moment to pay homage –
my slack shadow smouldering above the empty pews.

You are Wheeled into the Bright Sunlight

And ceremoniously the surgeon dons
his scrubs, the texture of bladder-kelp
strewn along the berm crest, thick
with beach hoppers and pill bugs known
to sting like needle-pricks. And in no time
you're walking across the sands to rock pools
in search of shrimps, lugworms and whelks.
And your Medulla, as predatory as anemones,
leads you to believe that the drill
boring a burr hole in your skull is the call
of curlews as the tide comes flushing in.
But your heart falters and you feel giddy
and strangely un-earthed. You stumble
to the cries of godwits and head throbs.
There is no choice but to leave your bones
for scavengers, and your desiccated skin
on hot stones. But always ready to make the best
of things, you take your chance. Never
a spendthrift of words, you hover over the spume,
mute, spreading your magnificent wings.

The Walled Garden

The skin of the harvest moon – terracotta flakes –
spiked the fluted greens, like the notes
you played on the piano to exorcise your grief.

In the soft brace of air, cabbage whites
fold their wings to pale green, slight
on the bramble blossom and apple leaves.

Here, there's an endowment of stillness to ease
your heavy ache for love. Stepping over pools
of broken glass, you look up to the windows

of the house, where the living, vacant and gaunt,
watch your shadow spill over the lawn and slip
through the wrought-iron gates.

Easter Gathering

Blood
dark as peonies
corresponds with this moment –
glossed rust-rain on the window panes
little gorged purses
of infinity, buttoned
by stars, confront this mouth
cavernous, full of moon spittle,
rich as loam, opening
and closing
practising a slackness, loose-muscled
for birth. And nothing
nothing to do with my foremothers'
obsessions – balm
roped hands, vinegar-soaked poultices.

I remember them –
mealy mouthed women
their gifts of salt, stolid
starch-breasted in their righteousness,
the way their collusive ringed hands
denied me.

Grandmother Cash

When the world was in a furore
of jack-boots and a ballyhoo
of bulletins cast from the fogged up
wireless, my grandmother beat
her disgust into the apple batter
and stalked off to the orchard
her fruit crop held like a gun.

Invisibly she could kill –
skin the big buck's bell with her slim bone knife,
her hands and forearms
steeped in blood, while I held my breath,
leaned away, tip-toed for flight.
And when she was cross,
I bristled like gooseberries
and crouched low, flat-backed,
like a natterjack in the damp
artichoke patch.

Her favourite word was *presently*
against which I was propped.
Portly she was not – no, not that
cushion-you-to-her-soft-bouncy-bosom
sort of grandmother. Her chest
was like a ladder-back chair
with no bulge for a heart.

Some years later, she surprised me.
When her only son was killed,
she took me to the very edge
of the beetroot field and called
his name to the setting sun.
I saw it dissolve to a crimson pulp,
brownly flecked, like rotten fruit.

Billet Doux

It was a place of unease –
feet fidgeting under desks
scored with love hearts and arrows,
bearing names of those long gone
who have endured.

That morning, Sir, flinty in his grey suit,
gave out the world news, his voice
spiking the barricades with a final
call to prayer – *Hands together, eyes closed* –
that little implement of debility
mingling with catkin dust –
while secretly small hands,
hot of impulse, set to work.

The boy's people
up from the river Wandle
stationed at their posts,
passed a note to the back of the class,
one shaping it into a paper missile,
darting over the freshwater meadows,
loaded with his declaration of love
for the girl with flaxen hair,
her Forget-me-not eyes tracing
its fall into the hollow of her lap,
slight as an orchid butterfly.

The Excursion

The train beat the track
like a tin drum, whistle hooting,
farmhouses bobbing on streams of green.
A breeze from the open window
played with her hair, sweeping down
a silky weave across her sleeping face.

Then, a new rhythm rocking to sea –
diddle-de-dee
diddle-de-dee ...
and I, too, fell to dreams
of unicorns and brindled cows,
woke to catch the bold brush strokes –
a fox in a sun-soaked field
where angels scythed golden wheat.

Gathering speed we flooded estuaries
and the sky was all watery and alive
with dolphin dances till a tunnel
swallowed us whole – belched up
and beached my mother and me
at Brighton Station. From the top
of the street, the sea was high as houses
and hand in hand, sleepily,
we went down and down

the sun, boiling the sky
to a froth of milk. She lay
in the blue-striped deckchair,
eyes closed. And the beach stones
clacked and clagged all day.
She was my friend no more. I sulked
at the sea's edge, pushing
back waves with my scraggy feet.

Waterfall

Fear strikes a single note on the piano. Its mesto
resonance falls into the white space of silence.
We must leave the house, but no reason why –
only shoes on with backs crushed, my coat belt
a tail between my legs. I follow her downhill
and we stop by the railway wall, smell its dank breath.
The rain fizzes like acid eating into something alive.

Too dangerous. Don't talk. A man, familiar in a dark coat,
passes on the other side and turns into our unlit house.
My mother grinds the back of her hand into her mouth.
Trees shake off their excess in one gust of wind.

I pretend we want for nothing. I pretend we're standing
under a waterfall, a forest mist caressing my face.
A van passes and then a boy with a hood. He mounts
a clapped-out bicycle, rides no hands. *Show off!* I shout.

Gold

Teacher insisted silence was golden.
In church, the Madonna wore a diadem of gold.
Her head bowed in supplication and devotion
my mother disavowed when she wrenched
her wedding ring from her finger and slipped it
into the rent-jug with payslips and pound coins.

I saw the moon, a splinter of mellow gold.
But it was fool's gold, more of a buttercup yellow.
I liked the lozenges of the parquet floor
in the school hall where we sat cross-legged
in the sunshine of a burnished forest
making liquid the sheen of Mansion polish.

A man from Galway made me a stool
from solid oak and sanded it, he said, to the gold
of bees' knees. Once, I dreamt it grew into a tree,
my room alive with goldfinches and leopards.
But from the buttery insides of my pencil box,
up wafted grandmother's apple store and brimstones
burrowed in the sunlit thatch of her hair.

The Quiet Man

His ailments she could cope with.
But when he started acting strangely,
goose-stepping along the hall,
reporting in the early hours
on the full and half-moons,
she said, *I'm at the end of my tether*.

He didn't want to go.
But he let the two men take him.
He told her: *Small streams have the real power*
because they replenish the sea.
Then he sat silently,
slumped in the ambulance.

One night, when the other patients
were asleep, he climbed out of bed,
threw flowers from vases
over sleeping heads, clawed
at the curtains, bellowing
and cursing till the nurses came.

She was so ashamed when they told her.
He was such a quiet man, all his life.

She sat with him for days,
his hand still warm
and soft inside, like the belly
of a newly born animal.

When he lifted his head
to look for her, she leaned
closer to hear his last words:
Remember, I loved you.
Now call the police.

Persephone

Mother is my only survivor.
Face grey as an egg,
she talks to herself
in her high-rise flat
thrust above bird-flight,
the Lambeth sprawl.

Come spring,
I must go to her. I am by now half-crazed,
dangerously thin.
I bring her gifts –
purple hyacinths
and pale primroses tangled in willow roots
I tore at, dragging myself
from the eddy and swirl
of the estuary.

She spies me through the peephole,
afraid of muggers, degenerates –
entanglements.

Unkempt
in my old bridal dress,
traces of algae on its damp silks,
I lift my winter veil,
whispering her name
again and again
to her blue, unconsoling eye.

Chagall's Midsummer Night's Dream

The sky is full of saffron seed
whirling and winnowed by the devilish
wings of an angel, red as ripe peppers –

and there in a puff of emerald cloud
sits an elfin clown, his fiddle tinged
with gold dust, smiling benevolently

at the bride, who gazes out of the dream,
her lips cut to a perfect almond closed on
perfection of dreamy love. Her dress

is smudged with earthy browns from
the groom's damp coat, wheat chaff
flecks the folds of her veil, and blue veins

bleed across her white sleeve from the bluest
of trees. She has given up her bouquet
of summer flowers for an open fan she holds

demurely across the groom's telling loins.
So we know she is not oblivious to his lurid,
hungry eye, but like the dreamer, we're

helpless to tell her of his coarse, goat skin,
prominent horns and how the clown's smile
has grown slaked and sinister.

The Woodshed

In the doorway, I heard
the wings of a heron
pass over like cool water.

The silence afterwards
made the air thick, just breathable.
I was in the woodshed again,
full of dead things – tinder-dry
seedpods baked black,
corpses of summer's bees
among rust-furred nails, and moths' wings
powdering along the sills.

Among his abandoned tools,
the old garden fork, rake and trowel,
my eyes widened for a sign –
a footprint in the dirt,
his thumbprint in the grey dust whorls,
a scratched line of scripture,
a holy word scored in wood.

I stood quiet and still,
as he would have liked me –
helpless in the space he had left
without knowing my place
in his dark scheme.

Plums

Sophie-Agnes, afraid of intruders,
took to her bed to hide from death
under the dark lid of her eye, slyly aslant
to catch the shadow totems of the forest
on her wall, her feet among the fallen leaves,
her head on tussock grass, a blade
between her teeth crushed sweet.

It suits her to believe I'm nine years old,
able to reach the latch without a step stone,
braid my own hair, stir the stew-pot of mutton bones,
life spilling out of me like the milk of dawn.
But she treats me like a disaster, like her
over-soft plums, slit by wasps, going to waste.

Years ago, she set her clocks to her own
diurnal rhythm, twenty minutes
ahead of meantime, wanderlusting
up the mountain side where I
skid on moss and sedge, and tumble down
into the baggy mouth of the wind.

Now, I lay her tray with its threadbare napkin.
A rose plate of shortcake, her little cache of pills.
A labour of love, these hands wind the clocks,
straighten the pillows, shake up the duvet.
I work a space for us in this fumy, heavy dusk.
No prayers or flowers, she says. *Promise?*
Afterwards, her dead weight in my arms.

Adrift

Stone effigies make their silent comment.
These are the supplicants, hands clasped piously
on breasts, their dresses and armorial suits
sculpted, peaked and crisp. No more stitching,
knitting, paring of bone needles, no bloody
battles, frost-bite, camping beneath stripped trees.

My ancestors sleep in no fixed abode.
Five miles from here a late London train
blurs under the bridge. I listen. Suck in
my own breath, rest the blades on the oarlocks,
holding them parallel to the surface of my thoughts
as the current carries me to the fields flat
as maps and roads rucked by tanks and trucks.

They want to transfuse my blood, these men in tents.
The wounded cry out for their mothers –
their country for a second chance. The needle
in, I trace the bloodline of my mother's name.
Her faint, unbroken signature leads me back
to the forest of black trees. Once more I'm
in the company of outlaws, whores and thieves.

Mina

Moonlight webbing gravestones.
A slumped figure in the graveyard,
her skin crêped, lap spotted with blood –
the bitter sweet offensive of his touch.
Bat-winged, he vanishes, the master of kitsch.
Poor girl doesn't answer to a name. Bogeymen
gibber and caper on graves. I lead her home,
sodden moss underfoot. A mist descends
and fills the room. I match her mental
wanderings – flash of a crucifix, garlic,
stakes, strands of her golden hair electric
in my hands. The fire is a lusting mouth.
She faints in rapture. Is this all a dream?
The doctor arrives. Opium golden-brown
and gritty from the phial. I rouse her
and feed her tiny portions, her lips suck in.
Then I turn the spoon and lick it clean.

Miracles

Your quiet settles like a mist over the days
we knew each other, when I watched you
slip denials into your pocket – a gatherer's hand
fisted against theft – against death and the clamour

of memories – wagons shunted into sidings,
hunger, the straw pallet and not forgetting the strange
alluring beauty of ugliness. It was without doubt
the time of clamped mouths when hands had eyes

and feet were booted and cloven. And yet
from within, love welled up and it was your damaged heart
that invented spring, bore witness to the first pin-pricks
of blossom on scorched stumps.

And the white starburst
of hawthorn worked its magic through the iron cold nights
and never went unattended.

Descent

He soon gave up his offering –
across the empty river, this quiet
ceremony of love, his white wings hollowing the air over hills,
and scars on his naked flanks,
like tattoos of rare orchids,
bear secret chronicles of the universe –
well, that's what they said.

Beyond lies a valley where craters once thickened with flowers,
where orchards of pippins and wild plum
dropped their fruits by his command.
I watched everything on the old brittle film
rattling the wheels of its projector. In black
and white on the outside wall, I saw his fall,
his immense body bringing heaven
down at his heels.

Afterwards, the moonscape of desert and rock;
dry seas slavishly tilted to earth, and the mind's circuits
fired up words, like sparks filed from stone of which
his bodyscape was made – the smooth hollow of his shoulder,
his profile broken in the half-light, and his eyes
wide open, flickering his own picture show.

Oxford Wedding

Who knows if it was an auspicious day.
The oracle was not consulted. We were
Beats, ultra-cool, existentialists wearing

our dead-pan, nonchalant masks.
Anyway, we took our chance –
you in your grey wool suit

and I in a cream Mary Quant –
the shade, they said, of a tainted youth.
I can't remember the shoes, but there

was your Ma and Pa and your giggling
sister, her hair scythe-sharp in a Vidal Sassoon.
And my mother, who always bore my

fads and whimsies with a quiet grace,
kept her distance as the sun dimmed
and the sky prepared for its blessings of

confetti and rice. And the trees along St Giles
spread their bare branches broadly for us
and we clattered up the wooden stairs

to the register office and huddled
in a cupboard space, where an old man
with a dry mouth read out the marriage vows.

I confess I would have vowed anything
to have you – which I did.
So, at last, the broad band of gold

sealed the deal.
And now to the kiss – ah –
sweet and potent like dark molasses.

I closed my eyes on it.

The Midwife

Attends me in the early hours,
her skin tight as caul, and I wonder
how it is that she seems so familiar
standing over me, her hair
a knot of vipers.

Now the blood rush, a deluge
of clotted words, and I lie motionless,
listening for the new-born cry.
But nothing – only scuttering in the dust
as she pins me down with her predatory
eye fixed on talons that clack on my
armadillo cuticles, probing my flesh,
turning me over, sacking my soft underside.
Soon the clamp over my mouth. The hiss of gas.

Afterwards, I wake to her sieving scraps
through her long fingers. Then, bent like a hoop,
she sweeps the floor clean of mud-scallops
made by the snouts of foxes who skitter
loose-limbed through this dreadful squandering.

Little Buddha

We are at peace.
It is an absolute, my love.

Your head is heavy
slumped against my cheek, downy

mole-nose
nuzzling your tight fist –

then a prim little milk mouth
silting up and surprising itself with a gulp.

I know my rocking and humming
are of no account – only the pulse

of a star will lull you to sleep.
I lay you down, little Buddha,

setting off on your trail of dreams.
Through your dark window, I see

a full moon caught in the black mesh
of the sycamore. There, a familiar

figure walks
along the furrows of the field

bending and rising, tending his snow-flowers.

Perspectives

Child, my friend of four,
has drawn a picture for my wall.

Look – an ostrich egg for a face
brimful of astonishment

and pin-head eyes squinting
beyond a whistle nose.

Blurred, I feel his little
finger-sprouts grope

for some touch, some presence,
and the reasons why this house

two-up and two-down levitates
with a pyramid roof,

and yellow waxed
sun-rays judder in a place

of nothing below a blue
cloudery ridge, and this

red caterpillar, most fiercesomely
moustached, impaled on spiked

grass, grins beneath the stony tree –
with cherries flat as planets – shaking

off an armful of black tangled
birds, squawking and angry.

Pouring from the door, a path
scoops the eye

up and up, high
to the gate in the sky –

Go, go, I say – follow.
But he, faintly scrawled,

recedes, goes deeper in
and in and won't meet me

in our destined space between.

Starlings

Sunday – feeling low – I'm at the sink
by the window, dunking knives and scraping

burnt gravy from the casserole. Little Sweetie
frets in her chair, mashed potato and carrot

bits in her hair. Latched to my hip
the baby frets, stretching for soap bubbles

as they crackle and fizz. Then, suddenly,
I'm running back to you, light years away

on Lambeth Bridge, as you saunter close
opening your army great coat to fold me in.

Another darkness swoops down, ruptures
and cleaves. Its shards scatter the dream.

Look, I say, on waking. *Look at all the birdies
on the lawn!* But to myself: how shrill

and raucous, yet lustrous – as beautiful.

Moondrop

That night
when I heard your cry, I
rose from my bed, groped for you
and pushed back the curtains in search of light.

There, the cryptic
script of black chimney stacks
and a full moon – a gilded O in the Book of Hours
luminous in its velvet pouch –
drew from you a deep sigh.

Your baby breath
popped in the arctic air.
You lifted your hand and pointed to the moon
and your first word –
a whispered ghost of a word –

hot

slipped through the window
and melted the glass.

Gravity

The chains jangle   the steel
links so fat   your fists
struggle on a grip   loop
those little   fat   grub thumbs
through the figure   of eight   there
now   shift   your bottom   into
the   soft dip   in the middle
of the seat   that's it   you're
ready   hold tight   off you go
up and up   higher and   higher
over the Thames,   over   the boats
over   Batter   sea power   station
look   see the swans   lust-rous
as milkglass   gliding   on the water
our   ha- ha-ha bounces   on   the
wind   ah no scissor-legs   work
them   together as one   lean
back   up now   down   whoosh
push   that tum-bum   away   from
from my hand   up   whee ee
down   again quickbend   those
knees   feet straight   breathe
please   whoop-ee   sun through
your eyes   hear   the chains   crash
up again   that's it   you're doing it
never   let go   keep your nerve
leave your   crushed smile   in the
blue   leaves   that's it   smash right
through   heaven   back to me
back to me

always

Fear of Sharks

We walk under the stars.
Look how they spin on their broad columns of darkness.

You can't tell me what I want to hear.
Our footsteps work to their own pace,
the way they once did when I took your hand,
plump and warm as a nestled mouse,
and led you home.

Now, as we walk without words, free
of their culs-de-sac and conundrums,
why is it I suddenly remember the way
you held your pencil (selected from the old *Roses* tin)
its point blunted from your frantic shading in
a love heart pierced by a red-tipped fin?

Wavelengths

In mid-winter dusk, we made our way
across Clapham Common – two exclamation marks

on a landscape of sculpted trees –
and bunched wires on plinths like minds

tuned into their own solitary circuit.
Then a roaring blast, and a train

shot from its hole to ravish the crowd.
After a quick embrace, I was on the train

leaving you on the platform, waving
at my fading smile. Ours was a separation,

a resonance from the heart, the way
a high-pitched scream can shatter glass.

And I remembered our game of hide-and-seek,
when you used to slap both hands to your face

in belief that if you couldn't see the world
then you, too, vanished without trace.

Blue Water Café

At first I thought you were dying –
piecemeal – in a kind of brooding.
Even your boredom was beautiful.

I watched you, lean and angular,
walk the shore, your eyes dancing on
the ghostly score of the Pacific roll.

And in the evenings you served me
cappuccinos with silver spoons –
told me tales about the Cockatoo Man

laughing feathers from his mouth,
honey ants and tall sea-eagle trees.
Stay, you said, *the dolphins come soon.*

But my feet pounded your song lines
North to Taree. And I'll never forget
how the moon scooped fruit bats

from the sky and Big Brother Mountain
loomed at the foot of my bed,
and the Great Rainbow Serpent

lay coiled on my pillow, while the echo
of your heels going home ruffled the kookaburra
strumming the wires, its cry naked and cold.

Elena

i
The first time I saw her
I was eating a peach
in the cool shade of the acacia.
She took the sour taste from my mouth,
three years old, dancing
along the shoreline
in a world of our own.

Her tripping feet had the cunning
of small animals as she leapt
and bobbed between the waves.
Her hair flounced and hugged her head
like a soft cloche.

ii
I saw a crowd gather round
a dead seal or shark. Clouds massed –
knuckle bones kneading the hills.

Closer, I saw a man
thump her bell chest and blow
his breath into her limp mouth.

A young woman knelt at her side
calling her name, and cicadas
drummed in the olive groves.
Gently, she thumbed open
the staring fish-eye. The sun
tunnelled in.
It touched nothing.

We stood
silent against the wind.
Too late –
her little fist-like heels

stubbornly dug in.

Awakening

Heaviest of afternoons
a woman draped in black,
her lap loud with ripe apricots,
drowses in the shade.

Cats laze, flat as pelts
stretched out on the veranda,
lined with scorched marigolds,
her dry bloodless geraniums.

Old Takis talks politics,
taps his stick, worries his beads.
I can smell apple on his breath
until a lapse of memory stifles him.

At last, dusk steals in.
The air is full again
with thyme, jasmine
and wild lemon-mint.

A breeze lifts the heat.
Cicadas sizzle to the gentle
counter-beat of the nightjar's note
rising coolly to its throat.

The woman wakes
passing you like a dark moth
on the path, and fireflies explode
from the old man's mouth.

You totter towards me
damp from sleep, brought to life
by a cracked moon strung up
like a piece of broken glass.

Night Watch in Prague

At his window,
he looks down on the city spread below,
a city spiked by spires and tramlines scoring cobble stones.
Roof tops rise and sag like hammocks
heavy, rimed with snow.

Unable to sleep,
he imagines those more fortunate. Their threadbare slippers
gaping on mats, soft eggshell breaking of embers
on the hearth, cast-off clothes fallen to the floor,
and coats frosting on hooks, abandoned
to strange distorted shadows.

And he contemplates how people might be found
asleep in the unearthly postures of the dead,
picturing their contortionist shapes set
in the soft gulch of feather beds, and infants
with arms and legs star-ward spread
like miniature Vitruvian men. And not forgetting
wide-eyed wives on their backs in the dark
listening for homecoming steps.

He glances over
to the Castle on the hill. It seems only
yesterday that he'd strolled, umbrella rolled,
his scarf crossed over his chest, and paused
to watch starlings perform their liquescent dance.
And then their final plummet to earth,
drawing down the last remnants of light.

Flux

Head cocked, this caught in a bird's nickel eye –
A woodland glade blazoned by the ebb and flow
Of its quicksilver warble. Below the spread
Of leaves, mercurial in the wind. The white
Skin of light flushes through the trees – trees
That know the weight of rain, scored ruts,
The slop and slither of mud – gliding torrents.
Vanishing to the underworld the waters hiss
And snarl, course through dark caves, loosening
The clench of roots in clay, and leave their legacy –
The beauty of ground leaves pellucid as streams,
And tree roots laid bare by the slack mouth
Of the mound, where sacred spirits sleep
And keep hold of ancient bones that shift and creak.

Aviator

I said I would go in place of his rowdy boys. The infamous
fall of Icarus with melting wings the great masters
dare not overlook finally persuaded him.

I flourished before him my sketches, of eagles in flight, bats' wings
and kites, and told him I, too, studied the movement of birds
under a Tuscan sky with my infant eyes.

I flattered him about the beauty of his inventions,
the hang-glider, the ornithopter, *The Annunciation,*
for the Portinari altarpiece – especially Gabriel's exquisite
wing formation.

In return, he showed me the grasshopper frame
whittled from pine, covered in raw silk, and the space
for me, his willing apprentice, to lie face down, my head
jammed in a device –

the crank and pulley for steering – where I was soon to witness
the world unravelling its blue thread below on my flight to
the Alps,
the wings vibrating like the strings of a lyre.

And on my return, my beak laden with snow, I'd let fall
to cool the bronzed heat of Florence. Such were our dreams.
Unrealised.
How we laughed, our heads filled with such foolishness and
feathers.

Daybreak

All night I struggled to rise.
Their stakes have me
pinned, taut between the sheets, my eyes
pressed back – two thumb pokes
in a head of clay.

I am exhumed daily –
a corpse wired to a humming bird.
In the small ache of sky
the sun appears – pink
fingertips as if someone
holds the cloud.

His yellow irises hang limp
over the rim of a metal jug.
If I lift my head a breath,
I can see the sea and remember
his promise to take me in
his rowing boat, and show me
how he feathers the oars.

Miranda and the Moon Calf

The ship leaves the bay with its precious load –
The child I loved, who was never afraid
To slip her hand into the paw of mine
And let me guide her to the brook
In the fertile grove of my Isle, when I
Was king and governed the sun and stars,
The wild waves, boar and deer and nightingales.
There we listened to the music of the wind
Of a thousand trees, leaves plucking the air
And the voice of Ariel wove a song
Through coral bone and the pearly conch
Of sea nymphs heralded our fables and dreams.

It was then I had shape, substance, the fragrance
Of earth in my veins, when my cries could
Lift the moon from her sphere, before the
Flesh-fly laid her eggs and hatched words
Loaded with shame, sin, curses, and man's
Bite tattooed my skin. And I am like water
In water, a drunkard, demi-devil, strange fish,
Finned, misshapen in the twinned globes
Of her abused eyes, and on land, left to crawl,
Dig pig nuts in the dirt and curse the tyrant
Who taught me his crimes, made a whore
Of my mother with his forked tongue, hissing
Like an adder to infect my ear. I will not go
To her country to be caged, prodded into
Madness as *a thing of darkness*, a monster
To gawp at, to writhe on my belly in filth.
Just as the spider wraps up the fly, so too
Will I capture her memory for eternity, curled
Like the secret nectar in the cowslip's bell,
For I am a sorry thing, yet free, in the windfall light.

Palimpsest

The sky is blue as a sparrow's egg,
inky trees painted in by Botticelli's ghost,
rosebuds retouched by his crimson brush.

Although time's grime is awash
over the meadows, in a babble of brick
ribs of memory bone through –

distant cruelties, histories too faint
to decipher now.
Shimmering in dark fumes

lorries claw the hill, hot
for the continent, and swallows cut
across the starved moon.

Who is able
will leave the gilded frame
before frosts break to metallic bloom.

Skylarks

The boy light as a bird
is lifted into the boat by the gunner
bristling for the kill. The boy's hand
placed on the rudder, the man at the helm
allows the boy to believe this is
what he must do to be among men,
steering the boat through spume
the fleet bobbing and tilting under
an uncertain sky darkened by a swarm
of migrating skylarks to winter in Africa.

The boy's eyes grow wild with the beating
of wings, the fusillade, the parched rainfall
of crying birds tumbling from his memory
as he stands an old man before Gozzoli's
fresco of St Francis blessing the birds.
And he recalls the dead kestrel with wings
stretched wide nailed to a crude cross
which made him scream in madness
to his mother's skirts, where he trembled
like the birds with broken wings.
And his mother called him Little Bird –
Little Bird who lived all his life
in this place of rage, this unblessed house.

The Blue Car and the Airstream Trailer

No-one seems to know
who cleared this patch in the woods
to bring the stone-blue winter light from the clouds
and claim for nature's own
the blue car and the airstream trailer,
their sensual curves and blue tints
polished to a silver patina by westerly winds.

Like metallic moon pods, they purr in sleep,
strike their spears deep into frost clefts
and await the arrival of the Apollonians.
Corrugated torsos and heads glassy
as fishbowls, they winter cocooned inside
the airstream chrysalis, and hatch stylishly in spring.

Their white gore crusts peeled away,
they emerge curiously human, taking off
in the blue car, impatient for city galaxies,
the sparking flints of fake stars, far from
their roots in the parched earth
and the first clean spill of summer rain.

Oversteps Books Ltd

The Oversteps list includes books by the following poets:

David Grubb, Giles Goodland, Alex Smith, Will Daunt, Patricia Bishop, Christopher Cook, Jan Farquarson, Charles Hadfield, Mandy Pannett, Doris Hulme, James Cole, Helen Kitson, Bill Headdon, Avril Bruton, Marianne Larsen, Anne Lewis-Smith, Mary Maher, Genista Lewes, Miriam Darlington, Anne Born, Glen Phillips, Rebecca Gethin, W H Petty, Melanie Penycate, Andrew Nightingale, Caroline Carver, John Stuart, Ann Segrave, Rose Cook, Jenny Hope, Hilary Elfick, Jennie Osborne, Anne Stewart, Oz Hardwick, Angela Stoner, Terry Gifford, Michael Swan, Denise Bennett, Maggie Butt, Anthony Watts, Joan McGavin, Robert Stein, Graham High, Ross Cogan, Ann Kelley, A C Clarke, Diane Tang, Susan Taylor, R V Bailey, John Daniel, Alwyn Marriage, Simon Williams, Kathleen Kummer, Jean Atkin, Charles Bennett, Elisabeth Rowe, Marie Marshall, Ken Head, Robert Cole, Cora Greenhill, John Torrance, Michael Bayley, Christopher North, Simon Richey and Lynn Roberts.

For details of all these books, information about Oversteps and up-to-date news, please look at our website and blog:

www.overstepsbooks.com
http://overstepsbooks.wordpress.com